T0324655

A HOG SLAUGHTERING WOMAN

The publication of this book is supported by a grant
from the Eric Mathieu King Fund of The Academy of American Poets

The New Issues Press Poetry Series

Editor   Herbert Scott

Advisory Editors   Nancy Eimers
                                 Mark Halliday
                                 William Olsen
                                 J. Allyn Rosser

Assistant to the Editor   Rebecca Beech

Fiscal Officers   Michele McLaughlin
                                 Marilyn Rowe
The editors wish to thank Douglas Ferraro for his essential
support in the establishment of this series.

The New Issues Press Poetry Series is sponsored by
The College of Arts and Sciences, Western Michigan University, Kalamazoo,
Michigan 49008.

The publication of this book is supported by the Arts Council of Greater
Kalamazoo through a program of The Michigan Council
for the Arts and Cultural Affairs.

ISBN: 0-932826-48-2 (casebound)
         0-932826-49-0 (softbound)

Library of Congress Cataloging-in-Publication Data:
Marlatt, David, 1963–
A Hog Slaughtering Woman / David Marlatt
Library of Congress Catalog Card Number 96-69692

Design: Tricia Hennessy and Brian Edlefson
Production: Paul Sizer
                    The Design Center, Department of Art
                    Western Michigan University
Printing: Bookcrafters, Chelsea, Michigan

A HOG SLAUGHTERING WOMAN

DAVID MARLATT

FOREWORD BY JACK DRISCOLL

New Issues Press

WESTERN MICHIGAN UNIVERSITY

For my Mother and Father

Contents

II

Foreword

Reading A Hog Slaughtering Woman is not unlike discovering a box of daguerreotypes in the attic of an abandoned farmhouse or barn loft. Portraits: Katherine Daley, Katie Teppe, Uncle Frank, Roy Nickol, Great Grandma Agnes who tossed "her slop pot / out the upstairs window every morning."

Preserved here is a community of rural folk whose histories Marlatt so fully imagines that each character steps magically from still-life back into this world where past and present co-exist, where a young boy, unable to fall asleep on a horse hair mattress, stays awake instead to watch "that mane / and tail hair / blowing . . ." Or in a poem that brings the generations together, that same speaker finds and puts on his "dead relatives' clothes," believing that he has "climbed into . . . and breathed a second life."

The language is deceptively casual, unhurried, idiomatic, humorous at times, witty, though always that conversational, anecdotal tone is set against a range of deeply affecting emotions: the speaker's eighty-nine year old grandfather, for example, in a poem both lighthearted and full of sadness, wanders off to the "long-closed depot to / meet great grandma," herself the victim of dementia. What these poems fight against is that loss of memory and, therefore, loss of history that betrays us. Marlatt knows that to remember clearly is to reenter the past, and to refashion it is his way of keeping it new and alive.

These are people who throw little out, who relink logging chains and seamstress their own dresses, and any one of the old and infirm characters might use a worn cornbroom rather than a cane or a crutch. They are poor but not poor in heart, and time after time the dilapidated landscapes of these poems are made beautiful by the clear-eyed rendering of simple details: the horses wearing fly nets, dahlias in full fall bloom along a cracked foundation, jars of gray peaches swaybacking the cellar shelves. Marlatt stays alert out of love, and it's this attentiveness to all that surrounds and grounds these poems that makes the lives of his people real and rich and enduring.

David Marlatt is a compassionate, formidable new voice, and embodied in this truly distinctive debut collection is a vision and maturity that I find rare, wise, and absolutely unpretentious. This is the kind of book I want to praise.

Jack Driscoll

Acknowledgments

Grateful acknowledgment is made to the following publications where some of these poems appeared.

California State Poetry Quarterly: "Winter Wool"

The Icarus Review: "Trout"

The MacGuffin: "Freight Jumper"

The Mustard Jar: "Mrs. Coughlin Talks of the Hoeskstra Roofing Company"

Nimrod: "Horsehair Mattress"

Passages North: "Mary Agnes," "The Saints' Cookbook"

Poetry Northwest: "A Hog Slaughtering Woman," "Snapping Beans with the Jehovah' s "Witness"

The PrePress Awards Volume Two: "Corduroy," "Spring Thaw," "Working Girl"

Sycamore Review: "Dahlias"

The Writing Room: "Before the Snow," "Katherine' s Hair"

I

Horse Hair Mattress

I could never sleep
on the horse hair mattress
in the back bedroom of my aunt' s house.
She carried me up the back steps afternoons
laying my wide child ears down
against the mattress ticking.
I could never sleep.
She told me
of Uncle Frank shearing
orange mane
from his matched chestnuts.
I rubbed my ear on the mattress
thinking only of Frank,
dirty hat on,
his own hair matted
against his scalp,
clipping handfuls of hair
with blunt-nosed
nickel-plated shears.
I knew he coiled the hair
in a burlap bag,
saved it
until there was enough
to fill a whole mattress,
but I could never sleep
on it. I kept thinking
of my aunt washing, soaking the mix
of mane and tail
in a galvanized tub
sudsed with the clear green
Superior cake soap Frank sold
in winter.
Spread on a sheet,

the mottled hairs reflected the sun.
I could never sleep
on the flattened hair
saved and packed tight
so many years.
I couldn' t sleep
with all that mane
and tail hair blowing
over those horses'
necks and backs
from one side to the other
cutting furrows up
cutting furrows back.

Kirby Vacuum Cleaner Repair and Sunday School

Inside, behind the burned-out maroon *Kirby* sign,
Carmen Salvagio hauls vacuum cleaners
onto his carpet-covered counter.

"I'll give you two dollars off the bill
if you can quote me two Bible verses."

My mother blinks her long black lashes
and snaps her purse clasp shut.
"How about an Act of Contrition," she says.

He spins the rollers, oiling the bearings,
and pops out the worn brushes
throwing them into a lint-filled bucket.

The Blessed Mother,
on a corner shelf
in blue and gold piping,
stares across a gleaming row of chrome-plated Kirbys
with her raised hands blessing
the rotted belts, cracked wheels, and blackened switches.

Carmen knows she's watching him work
and keeps track of his prayers,
fingering each black rosary bead
hanging in a greasy wad
in the lint of his pants' pocket.

One pocket for the rosary.
One pocket for his all-purpose miniature screwdriver,
Goebel's church key, and Saint Christopher medal.

"Read Matthew and learn two verses or more.
I'll give you a discount
on a bag or hose attachment."

Winter Wool

When I was fat enough to hold up the worsted threads,
I began to wear my dead relatives' clothes,
clothes my aunt, mother, and grandmother
saved in cedar chests; or carefully sealed in boxes under stairs,
or in the back of the attic.
I wore the sweat stains of men
I hardly or never knew,
and through the scent of soap
rolled in socks
I could smell the smoke
of unfiltered cigarettes as though
those men had just removed their woolens
in the spring thaw.
Smells of her men
filled the rooms of my grandmother's house,
filled the down tapestry chair,
handled the railing balustrades
downstairs into the kitchen
where I'm certain all that heavy wool
hung from the wooden backs of chairs
just short of shrinking above the floor register,
melting half-shoveled snow
from the cuffs of pants still sewn with suspender buttons.
One morning after a winter storm,
when I was ten,
my grandmother went digging, tearing into her hidden things,
and laid out two pairs of my uncle's shoes,
stained cordovan brown,
grey pants with the soft nap worn smooth in the knees
and a thick sweater of tightly knitted alpaca.
I climbed into that wool and breathed a second life.

Before the Snow

We call it a convention
when the birds come in the fall
filling the bare burr oaks
with thousands of fluttering black leaves.
They all move at once
from the shagbark hickory
that once shaded the Bissell schoolhouse.
Turning to the North
and back to the South
they head for the rotten spruce trees,
pulling carpenter ants
from split and cracked trunks,
bracing themselves against the wind
and stocking up against the flight.
Their chattering can be heard
across the stock pond
echoing off wide fence rows of maple trunks.
They've come to talk
about the nesting last spring
and whose blueberries they stole.
They stop
getting word of a swarm of gnats
warming themselves over Roy Nickol's manure pile.

Mary Agnes

Great Grandma would rather walk to church than ride
the 12 blocks in my grandfather's Ford.
There was no one who could force that woman
into that Ford. I mean no disrespect to my elders,
but George Jackson at Akin's Lumberyard said
she was crazy from too much child bearing.
But I never heard of such a thing before.
I don't know what anybody ever did
to get her that way,
whether it was bad bile or the chestnut spines
that always filled her yard.
She paid a man up the street 25 dollars
to cut down her chestnut tree. She couldn't
wait for the blight to kill it, stop it
from shedding its spiny hulls onto her lawn.
I overheard her say one Sunday afternoon
while turning the chicken over in the sink,
There never was one who did anything to please me,
the words muddled into the drain and chicken blood.
Wouldn't ever use the indoor bathroom my grandpa built.
Always used the backhouse, and I suppose she did
go off base tossing her slop pot
out the upstairs window every morning.
I don't know why she was the way she was.
My own grandpa himself lost it all at 89 wandering down
to the long-closed depot to
meet great grandma.
He knew she would be mad
if he were late.

Boiled Coffee

Aunt Carol knew coffee
like nobody else.
Without having to think, she scooped
the ground coffee out of the can
mixing it with half a cup of water
and an egg white she separated
using one shell against another,
never mind getting a bit of shell in the coffee,
you weren't going to drink the shell anyway.
Pour in the water and set it to boil.
Pour in more water and let it warm
on the back burner awhile until it's done.
It must have been good coffee,
she always made it that way,
and everyone at her house
drank her coffee the way she made it.
I don't really know if it was good
or bad. I was young, bare faced
and didn't like coffee then.

Sheriff Kirby Mason, My Uncle,
and The Kalamazoo County Fair

In a photograph, my uncle is standing on the sand
at Oval beach, Lake Michigan.
He's slim, wearing a black suit and skinny
black tie. He's smoking
a cigarette on a late Sunday afternoon
squinting at the camera.
It's one of the few existing
photographs of my uncle.

Leaving the Kalamazoo county fairgrounds' North gate
he says, "Show Sheriff Mason your badge,"
a tin badge stamped from a fruit cocktail can
I won popping balloons with darts.

It's 28 years later and I'm still standing
there in the center of the midway
possibly throwing darts, tossing rings,
holding my uncle's hand while a red-faced
barker at the claw machines threatens
a stubble-headed kid with
a sledge handle. It's 28 years later

and the smell of the fairgrounds' vomit and the trough
urinals makes me pitch my uncle's pennies
higher into the stacked glassware,
just to bring something home,
the amber beer garden glasses.
The levitating Peerless valve
still runs water infinitely under the grandstands
into a bottomless barrel.
It's sulky racing in this unbearable humidity;
my mother and father sweat away, wearing square dance
colors. Bright bunting twirls in the exhibition tent.

If he hadn't been a school teacher, my uncle
would have bid on the Polish hens with
their full, brilliant crests, swine, goats, sheep,
angora rabbits all reviewed with equal care
as if he knew what he was looking at.

I can feel myself shift to the moving weight
of the turnstyle pony's shoulders,
the saddlehorn under my hands.
My uncle combs his thick lanolin-slicked hair with his fingers.

After so much time, I can't help but think
he was a sainted man,
mugging at me every time
my painted horse made its round
to the sound of the grinding calliope chimes.

The Summer of the New Well

The summer I killed my pet chicken
my sister milked cows

at Lockshores and my brother drove
a rusted-out truck for Terminix.

It was the summer I lit
a rolled-up newspaper to see the lock

on the upper hayloft door. My friend
Jeff said *This looks like a good place*

to piss and arched out the hatch
onto a dead lawn mower. That summer,

I sold squash alone, and my uncle started
a cough that didn't stop until January.

Nobody slept the week of his funeral.
Katie Teppe took a drink and said,

That's a damn nice looking coffin.
I dreamed of him lying in the coffin

wearing my father's hat and buckle galoshes.
The summer I killed my pet chicken

I swam a mile with my sister. She said,
Nothing lasts forever. Let's go fishing.

Jeff stole me a bottle of beer.
My grandmother put her hand on her hip

and said, *Get inside, your dinner's getting cold.*
The summer I broke that chicken's neck

my hair went curling in the rain, and a man came
to drill the well about 20 feet deeper.

Snapping Beans with the Jehovah's Witness

The long green stringless are wiped
clean in our dry hands and pop
easily into three sometimes four pieces adding
quickly to the winter's mound piled
on clean newspaper. A corroded galvanized bucket
slowly fills with stem ends and tail ends.

Rusted and rotted are tossed,
worm ends snapped off,
good ends saved.
Gram piles beans between her knees
on her wrinkled cotton dress
smudging the faded blue pattern.

She flips wet beans onto the papers,
glad as always to be busy,
to be working her hands.
Our necks turn up our rutted drive
to the well-dressed couple who decide
not to chance the lane with their Buick.

"How are you folks this afternoon?
Have you been saved by Jesus Christ?"
"Oh, for a good long time now.
You need a lift to the gas station?" says Gram.
I shoot a dry bean across the lawn.
"Do you ever read from the Bible?"

"Monsignor O'Brien never wanted us to,"
says Gram, smoothing her corduroyed lap
and dumping out a fresh pile
of sandy beans to snap.

"Have you heard of God's kingdom
on earth prophesied in Revelations?"

the man says, finding a finger-browned page.
The cats serpentine the man's legs shedding
onto the upturned creases of his cuffs.
"May we read you a passage from the Bible?" the woman says.
The beans still snap crisply
and Gram stands, remounding

halved beans on the classified section.
"If you'd like a ride to the gas station,
my grandson will take you, otherwise
don't just stand there,
help us with these beans,"
she says, and reloads her lap.

Molly at the Radio

Molly looks to the other side and seems to know
that she's lived far too long. She's still troubled
by the dry August heat reflecting in the screen door

off the brick street and says its slothful the way the chickens go
around unfed for weeks at a time. She thinks it's awfully late
in the year for horses to be wearing fly nets.

Sorting, creasing the folds in that same grey apron, she looks
out her good eye, smells the pigs across the dried-out river
and turns on the Motorola at elbow.

"Land sakes, people ought to stay shy of airplanes."
She is 102, tells me I'm too tall, "Put a brick on your head.
I can't see past you." She is 102,

laughs at my dog licking her knee,
hooks her hair behind her ear,
plays with a string of pink glass beads,

and scoots around the house holding an old oak rocker.
Last Fourth of July, she gave me five dollars
to buy firecrackers.

Mrs. Coughlin Talks of the Hoekstra Roofing Company

Don't step on the grass
in your bare feet.
The roofers left nails
and cedar splinters across the lawn.
He must have been tight.
They were all tight.
I expected them to fall through
the ladder rungs or tip,
loaded lopsided, off the eaves
with those shingle bundles.
Even the cats knew it was dangerous.
They were all drunk,
and I don't know why they didn't have the sense
to bring their own ladders
instead of climbing those paint-splattered things we got.
Didn't even put the first row on straight.
You'd think they could have got that right before they even got
        started
drinking and carrying on.
That damn chimney's tilted enough without them
leaning on it. How do they get away with it
anyway? Think they'd know better
than to get their necks broken.
I said, 'If you do break your necks,
it's no fault of mine. You've got no reason
to be up there, three sheets to the wind.'
But they did it anyway, and it's no wonder
you can't walk across the grass here without any shoes on.
They didn't rake a damn nail.

Working Girl

If I said I once loved a girl who stacked
firewood close under her chin, I would say more.
That it was the deftness of her steps over
uncut branches and chips
to stack each piece of stovewood
that drew me close.
Her father cut stove-lengths
across a circular blade.
She turned her head away
from sawdust blowing in the near-winter wind,
settling on her wool hat and lashes.
They knew it was too late in the year to be
cutting stovewood from fallen old-growth,
but her father cuts while the gasoline holds out
and her own untiring hands curl at the wrist to carry
every new length to pile against the snow.
If I said that I loved her,
I would say that I loved her from that moment
I saw her sweating in the oversize
of her brother's worn workcoat.

Bruise Blood

The first time my sister was kicked
by a horse she pulled down her pants
and showed half her hind-end.
It was a clear blue-blackish hoof-print
surrounded by a bloom of yellow,
and I swear I thought there was some green
in it as far as I could see.
She wouldn't let me touch it.
In the bruise, I saw the kick,
full strength of hind quarters
and back-stretched hock
that hit and spun her
so fiercely she got up a stunned distance away
in the April mud, on all fours,
and started to breathe again.
Before she could even stand,
she lay on her side flexing
her knee to her chest and back straight
to see if it would all still hold together.
I touched the bruised imprint
with an empty soup can
filling the inside of the blue hoof.
What did you do to him, I said.
Turned my back on him, she said,
shoving my shoulder.
Not a thing, she said, *not one thing*.
'*What'd you do to him.*
What'd you do to him,' she said,
and buckled up her belt.

Christine's Second Wreck

It seems like I'm always going to tow yards
to look through wrecks,
my father's Falcon sedan, Gram's Dodge, Christine's Ford.
The wrecks are indistinguishable behind the rust
bleeding through the repainted chain-link fence.
This time the yard is complete with a brown and black mongrel,
bred by other yard dogs in the salt-weathered street.
Sleeping under a truck bed, he's ready to grab any
fence climber by the pant leg.
The guy with the keys hops out of a truck,
wades through his pants pockets to unlock the gate
and waits, carving work from under a nail. I think
some of these cars were in the same wreck, and I'm tempted
to piece together each car to recreate the accident,
morbidly joking about the drunk
who never took his foot off the accelerator. I'm sick,
looking for my friend's car to see how bad she took it,
and when I find it, I know she's much tougher than I,
the resilience of her blonde hair instantaneously molded
against the windshield and the spreading star of glass
that would have killed me.
In the glove compartment are some outdated maps,
fuses, and a Saint Christopher medal. I had asked
if there's anything she might want. Is there anything
she might need. There really is nothing to keep from a wreck,
but we need them, the maps and medal.
They're the only things friendly and familiar in the yard grass
burnt with spilled gasoline and coolant.
We want them for the next car, but
in the middle of the kitchen table
they're dirty and so unfamiliar.

My Father's Apprenticeship

In the carpenter gang, a boy of fifteen cleans lumber,
pulling bent nails from wrecked planks
with the worst hammer, nicked so bad
they call it a farmer's hammer.
He sorts out usable lengths from splintered scraps
that go to feed the shop stove all winter.
In winter or rain, an apprentice learns to sharpen
the fine alternating teeth of a crosscut saw and
runs the chisel bevel on the face of the Arkansas stone
until the mirror edge curls back
hair-sharp as the iron of a plane.
He handcranks the grindstone while old man
McGaffan sends sparks
across the room where on a bad day
my father might stand at the anvil
and hammer straight a can of bent nails.

Bruce

Bruce looked like an old man. He had such a soft voice. I didn't think that seemed to fit him. He didn't look like he should be named Bruce, either. I don't like the name, so I guess nobody looks like Bruce to me. I first met him in the middle of the night. My friend Joe told me that his brother was a sworn addict to weed and that their father had once offered him $1, 000 dollars if he'd cut off his braids. He had two, one for his head and one for his beard. Joe said Bruce hadn't cut his hair since 1971. I didn't exactly believe that he braided his beard when Joe told me. When I met him, he was smoking a cigarette next to his van. It was dark, and every time he lit a smoke I looked quick to see the braid under his chin. I asked him a lot of questions just to be friendly-like and interested. He said, "What are you doing? Writing a book?" I was drunk. I asked, "Is there still a bounty out for your hair?" He said, "You want a smoke?" It was a Chesterfield, and I smoked it down quick so I could bum another and get a good look at his beard when I lit up. He mowed lawns for a living. He mowed to fish. Working on the lawn mowing crew, he was assigned the weed whacker. They called him Whacko, which I thought was a much better name than Bruce. I liked it. I didn't like Bruce.

Spring Thaw

Streams of rust
run off the broken hinges
nailed tight to the old man's shed,
waiting for the long dead smith in Cressy
to mend the halves.
There are other things too,
like hitch bolts and bicycle chains,
that put back together could always be used for something.
But the smith's dead,
buried up on the graveled hillside in Cressy,
surrounded by twisted shafts,
peened and drawn to hundreds of sharp points
around that untillable hillside.
He's dead and he's been dead
and so is just about everybody else
who ever brought a horse to be shod
or logging chain to be relinked.
But still the old man saves everything in bundles,
in boxes, in crates, and barrels,
for another depression, another life,
for his son in Chicago to turn the burdock and sumac sprouts
in the spring.
But the boy's had enough summers
of twine burns behind a stationary baler,
and trips to the elevator scoop-shoveling corn
into the spiraling auger of its bottomless grate.
He'll never be back.
The cans pile up outside the rotting threshold
in bulging burlap bags.
The old man stuffs rags in broken window panes.
The whole place will burn one morning
sealing the bargain in a handshake of flame
while he's on his knees
lighting the stove.

The Saints' Cookbook

My great aunt keeps holy cards in her purses,
dresser drawers, hat boxes.
Some of the cards are edged in a layer
of gold, and some saints are haloed in gold
against blue-grey clouds.
Wedged in the frame of her etched glass window
is Saint Jude, the patron of hopeless causes,
and at the kitchen sink she prays
to get her father out of the purgatory
he wandered off into.
She scrubs potatoes clean
and breaks off their tangled, sprouting eyes.
Holy cards mark recipes in *The Saints' Cookbook*.
Saint Theresa the Martyr Casserole:
3 diced potatoes
2 cans tuna fish
3 Hail Marys
1/2 cup condensed milk
She fills her own holy water font,
an empty vinegar bottle
she takes with her to church,
but the water won't last
until the blessing at Easter.
Every night she keeps her upper sash open
so an angel can come
and take her home, sleeping
in her own coarse wool.

II

Corduroy

I have a thing for watches
She has hair like dark varnished walnut
I smell ground lavender blossoms
She combs no tangles out
I smooth it with my hands
She wears worn corduroy
I fasten the dried leather buttons
She finds that she 's quite self-reliant
I wrap her in tight knitted wool
She smiles when she's washing the dishes
I find she collects small bones
She sits in the sun with no hat on
I think she keeps small bones on the lower sash rail
She digs in the garden with a shovel and a spoon
I rake the grass into rounded-up mounds
She says she's going for a walk
I varnish the croquet mallets
She picks winter apples
I paint the boards white
She still sits in the sun
I have a hat on
She hates splattered paint
I don't wash it off
She blisters away on the unmown grass
I haven't raked of fallen new growth
She cups acorns in her hands
I look at the time on the face of my oiled wrist-watch
She winds the stem and sets the time slowly
I find that she's most appealing
She smiles when she's washing the dishes
I ask why she smiles
She says she's thinking of corduroy in winter
I never protest when she's washing the dishes

She gathers winter apples because they are hard
I like them because she likes them
She never heard a peacock crow
I knew a farm in Iowa that raised them
She never was interested in that story
I rang her up several times on the telephone
She talked very quietly for a very long time
I told her that I like corduroy in winter also

A Hog Slaughtering Woman

1.

When Frances Woodburry ran her dark Falcon sedan
head into our loose hog, it was a hot day not given
to idle talk or the shuffling of papers.

2.

Frank moved from his down print in the tapestry chair
more excited than when the piano tuner came
wobbling a wrench and spreading a hand to strike

3.

intervals that echoed, attenuated seamlessly through
the ductwork and pipes, through the screen door
all over the yard.

4.

My mother was not sorry, save seeing
blood puddled under the burr oak, acorns
washed in the long wind-turned grass.

5.

I had never seen Frank's blackened hams hanging in the cellar
    must,
high to the floor joist from a spike,
tied, bound by several twists of twine.
His curing days of rubbing in salt and smoking were over.

6.

If he had planned the afternoon, it would not have been as good,
a heavy woman from up the road bending to butcher
a hog in the side yard, the concave chrome of a Falcon's bumper,

7.

an old man sharpening and resharpening knives
against the bone, against the sound of oil and stone.

Killed Out of Season

In forty acres my mother rents to Jim Campbell,
two men are chasing a deer running
on three legs, one leg obviously splintered
by the two tail lights beside the twisted
Osage hedge that won't keep anything off the road.
The men, one with a cap, the other bald,
flank both sides of the deer making it bolt
one direction and collapse the other.
It rights itself in the cut stalks
and heads south toward the house
until it falls, rights itself, and falls
again jerking like perch on ice
while the man in the cap unclasps
a knife and the bald man holds the deer's
head down. They cut the throat and run
for the house to use the telephone.
They must call the sheriff
to take home road kill.
Through the Osage hedge, I can see them
gut out the meat and sign the papers.

Katherine's Hair

I once saw my grandma with her hair undone.
It was long, white and wild.
Wind blew it about as she leaned on a dying elm.
I'd seen her first communion picture,
dark brown pipe curls
overflowing her shoulder
onto the white, gathered dress
Aunt Kate made.
Her eyes are the same.
"Oh, don't look at me, " she said.
The wind blew from the East
shooting maple seeds,
pulling long strands
across her face.
With both hands,
she gathered her hair
from the wind,
caught it up
with Ceylonese combs
carved from ivory

Fruit Stripe Zebra

This afternoon when I was buying gas, I picked up a pack of Fruit Stripe gum. I saw the zebra on the package and remembered that if I was going to start to chew, I should buy another pack because the flavor doesn't last too long, and the aftertaste is bad. The zebra on the package also reminded me of my Uncle Bob. He would send in for every free offer advertised on the backs of boxes and labels. We had a whole set of Campbell's soup bowls that my uncle sent away for after saving labels for over a year. The next year we ate enough soup to send away for the mugs. Bob ordered cat calendars offered by Little Friskies and Puss 'N Boots. If my cousin liked a cat picture for a particular month, my uncle would leave the calendar on that month for the rest of the year. We got free catfood and water bowls from Purina. There were red and blue checks on the sides of the bowls. There was the Kitty Self-Serve food-and-water-bin. The cats ate all the reserves at one time, and the inverted water reservoir filled the bowl and kept right on running onto the porch floorboards. One summer my cousin and I got Fruit Stripe zebras in the mail. My zebra was all flattened out from being stuffed into the corrugated cardboard mailing box. It had green felt ears and a black felt mane, google eyes, green, yellow, and red stripes, and a braided black yarn tail. I liked it better than anything else we ever got because my uncle carefully saved and divided the gum wrappers so my cousin and I could each get a zebra at the same time.

Painting Shutters

The summer came when
my Uncle Bob painted the shutters.
Forty-two windows on my grandmother's old house.
Two shutters to every window makes
eighty-four shutters in all to scrape and paint.
Half had already dried and shrunk so bad in the sun
the frames opened, with the rain
running through them,
and the slats fell into the day lilies
under the front windows.
The whole summer he spent the afternoons
carefully lining up the slats, gluing
each piece into the weathered frames.
He wore out three steel-bristled brushes from Dorgan's
hardware store scrubbing his own peeling coats of black
down to the chalky green my grandfather brushed on
40 years before.
One Sunday afternoon in August
Bob set the ladder on the sawhorses and leaned
each shutter against it to be primed black.
He never finished a day's work
without Gram calling him in
and putting newspaper on the back of his chair
or under his feet at the kitchen table.

The job never did get done, and after he died
my brother and I climbed the ladder with the broken rung
to hang the shutters that he did finish
for that job that never did end.
Two shutters to each window,
hinged on the house, rotting before we could reach them.
The next winter, the ladder with the broken rung
lay out behind the shed, covered with leaves, snow,
the melt-off flushing the downspouts
washing over and over onto the rotting rungs.

Martin O'Keefe

The hired hand this year like last
mixes his gravy with green beans
dabbing them on his fork with a folded slice of bread.

The week's meals are on his napkin,
tucked in under the worn cloth of his collar.
Chin bent to his chest, he waits
to eat while Kate and Frank cross
themselves and say grace over the gravy.

His hair, slicked with lanolin, shows the wave
where his hat worked all day.
He puts dollar slices of beets
on his mashed potatoes. The purple juice
curdles the gravy and stray peas.
He stirs them together, smashing them
flat on the back of his fork.

They are done for the day,
and after dinner, Martin and Frank
have a smoke, take off their shoes,
shake out the dirt
of another day's work.

Freight Jumper

In Holyoke, Massachusetts, there was no one, not even his sister
making eyes at Francis O'Brien, that could keep
my grandfather from riding the freights
across the Connecticut river, from one side of the mills
and back, on the rails all day.
As long as the mills kept spinning,
there was nothing that could keep his hands
in the bottom of his pockets
when steel and the tendered sulfur smell of steam rattled
the ground.
In that pulp town,
my grandfather Coughlin would rather
the wheels had cut his leg clean off.
A photographer in Poughkeepsie
leaned the boy with his pipe curls
and mangled leg against a wicker chair
for the family photograph,
brothers James and Kerwin brandishing new derbies,
hands on his shoulders,
pinkies fingering his celluloid collar.
I'd seen him bend in the garden,
leg stiff in front of him,
while he tamped in onion sets,
and I'd seen him clutch the Ford plunging
all the weight of that leg onto the pedal.
But I never saw the scars
or the Civil War surgeon who mended the crushed pieces
into a kneeless trunk.
Even then the doctor must have been too old
remembering mortar shells and mill accidents.
He was old enough
to know that a boy, a freight jumper,
needed two legs to live
in a town of mills and trains.

Katherine Daley Has Reached Her Prime

Kate was not one to worry about giving offense
when she would squat in the yard, at her age
of eighty-two, to work loose the full root
of a dandelion marring the uniformity of the grass.
No one would cross her because they knew she did
as she did for no other reason than the job needed doing.
As if the work was just waiting for her,
she would not worry about the near insult
and head out to pull weeds beside a neighbor's
front steps. The neighbor, equally proud of her own
housekeeping, would say, "You know you don't have to do
        that," or
"I've been thinking about digging that thistle all week."
The family on her side is like that, my grandmother said,
especially those whose hair is red.
Her pride and the early greying of her beautiful red hair
cast the sharp tone of Katherine Daley,
my grandmother said of her own aunt.
I could not fault Kate, who I never really knew,
when with her black walnut cane she poked
my mother and aunt, saying, "I never had good stout legs
like you girls," for I knew that her ability to squat
in the yard came from working in the fields at the berries
and beans another age ago when she burned
in the sun, and now she says as she pleases.
My mother said when Kate sold her farm the only things
she had left were some hats in boxes, a good cook stove,
a little money, and her collie,
Bill, who if he were here now
would still bring in the cows
if Kate called him to it.

Cistern

One summer my grandmother went cleaning
the swaybacked cellar shelves and sent
two dozen jars of grey peaches

shattering down the cistern's
inside plastered wall before
my aunt made her stop. Sometimes

in the spring thaw, the cistern works.
Clogged gutters and drains
give way to a flood from the roof

of leaves, sticks, bark, dead birds;
and winged seeds find their way
from the silver maple

whose straggling roots grow in
under the porch, poke through
the cistern's brick and plaster

looking for a drink.
Capillary hairs hang there waiting
for some summer storm,

or late fall rain to raise the water high
enough to offer a drink, to wet
the pump's cracked leather tongue.

The Mail Carrier

One year our mail route driver, Earl Jackson,
got his picture in *Life* Magazine.
There was a big picture and lettering.
"Earl Jackson Swears by his Plymouth
Driving over 50,000 miles a year
on his RFD route."
It looked like Earl all right
with packages, and letters all stacked up on the dashboard,
steering wheel with his canvas gloved hands gripping it,
hat brim flipped up
and him smiling with his crinkled eyes so you could see
all the fillings in his molars.
We sat around the kitchen table
talking about whether Earl really drove 50,000 miles a year.
If he drove 70 miles a day, six days a week,
that wouldn't add up to 50,000, now would it?
He never went anywhere else,
just drove the route
and watched the fluid levels.
But it sounded like something he'd come up with.
The post office warned him that his habit of driving
in the gravel on the wrong side of the road
was an unsafe practice.
My father said Earl used to sell bottles of bad gin
from the back of his car during prohibition.
My father said if you could flag him down in those days,
you could buy a bottle and a joke that he'd tell
everybody else before
not quite so easily letting his foot off the clutch.

The Mower

Bruce mowed to fish. I saw him bare-chested mowing grass by the iron gate outside the McInerny's place. He said he knew a stream where the trout were thick in the water, but he wouldn't tell me where it was. I said, "Let's go for some beer." He had to mow. The next time I saw him he was shoveling walks at the school. He said it was pretty good for perch up at Au Gres. He was looking forward to smelt dipping. I saw him at the pier in Frankfort thread a worm like my mother tying off a hem knot. He tied a brass swivel on his line. I never saw him without his canister of coffee and the never-ending stream of tobacco smoke that yellowed his beard. "Four dollars gas, pack of Winston's, and a dozen crawlers." He gave me a ride to Joe's house in his van. Those were his staples for a drive, coffee in hand, a smoke, and cups of crawlers in the back. I didn't see him again until the next summer. He was mowing medians for the city. He said, "I caught a 14 pound brown last weekend at the Boardman."

"You got any pictures?"

"I ate it," he said, and pulled the mower's cord.

Clarence Bender

He sits silently
in his striped overalls.
The good ones.
Wisps of white hair shoot off
his bald head.
Wide, freckled forearms
grasp the arms
of the green vinyl chair.
My aunt, Big Blanche,
goes to talking.
Quietly he polishes the sweatband
of his salt-stained fedora.
He reaches over his fat gut,
puts on his cap-toed shoes.
A frayed Panama replaces his street hat.
A hoe kept shiny so the dirt falls off
is his cane.
"Peas, beans, tomatoes."
He leans on the hoe in monosyllabic conversation.
"Don't step on the vines, son."
Clarence's garden.
The cover of a Burpee catalogue.
No sign of chick weed or Creeping Charlie.
I talk.
He lets me.
Nods his head.
Feet sink ankle deep.
Swaying up the backsteps
past the everyday overalls,
he changes hats.
Big Blanche on the kitchen stool
starts to talk again.

Clarence finding a chair
falls into the background
watching through clouding eyes and wire glasses.
Arms crossed
in his deaf world.

Katie Teppe After Sunday Dinner

Through the overgrown and broken Northern Spies
Mrs. Teppe drinks beer from brown long-neck bottles.
Acorns gather on the hood of her car.
She dropped in after the mashed potatoes.
"I haven't heard you play piano in years, Mr. McBride," she says.
My Aunt Carol clears the keyboard
of yellowed books and Christmas cards.
Slaughter On Tenth Avenue warms Uncle Bob's fingers.
Gram breathes a Manhattan
and holds up the end of the piano.
"Katie, old dear, we've got to sing."
Inside the citronella-painted screen
they flip through ripped stacks of sheet music.
Roses of Picardy.
They loller the words.
Smoke yellows the wallpaper.
Aunt Carol and my father jitterbug on the kitchen linoleum.

Wild Leeks in the Hedgerows

I asked him what
the hell he thought he was doing
knocking apart Hobart's silo.
Concrete tiles cracked and shattered into pieces.
I remember Hobart filling his silo for his cows in the winter.
It stood there a long time after he died
and the world almost seemed the same,
even though the cap fell in.
The guy said it was dangerous and he'd likely get sued.
I walked back to my own house
across the stubble field of harvested soybeans.
He doesn't know what to do with a place,
a house, where a woman named Ruth
pulled horseradish roots that grew
around the water spigot.
Fumes from her grinding the root
would make your eyes water.
I could never drink from the spigot,
thinking of her eating horseradish by the spoonful.
Hobart shot stray dogs chasing his sheep,
cauterized the bloody castrated lambs
with a glowing soldering iron.
I rode on the footboard of his Farmall
with three moldboards cutting and turning
deep furrows in the blackest dirt in the county.
Now this guy puts aluminum siding
over the narrow clapboard.
I never see him outside to look for wild leeks in the hedgerows,
as Ruth had done.
He sold off the south field in residential lots.
Landscapers roll down sod
and haul away the topsoil in orange trucks.
One winter Hobart cried when so many ewes aborted,
covered his eyes with canvas gloves,
yelled at me to go home.

Carp

When the sun begins to burn the night wet from
the thousands of backlit grass-woven spider webs
drying past dawn, the carp feed
so close to this dammed
river that if you were still enough,
and had the mind to,
you could hand-feed their o-ring
lips when they surface and suck,
but that's nighttime feeding.
At midmorning, before a line is wet
or a boat is launched into draft from the weed-edged
ramp, if you had the mind to, you could
crouch or squat near the water's
edge to stroke a carp's dorsal
fin for a moment before
it lurched and sent the other
feeders churning the slow current.
When they ask at the park gate
if there's good fishing in the river,
I don't mention the carp but
the pike, walleye and bass.
I don't want to admit to their
quantity, that I cut them loose
from abandoned stringers,
that they are caught and tossed
to the weeds and raccoons,
that I've seen them
in the heavy sludge of paper mills,
piled like fieldstones before the dam's brink.

Bruce and the Bluegills

Bruce did-in 24 bluegills with a big spoon
from the kitchen drawer that night.
I said, "How do you know if you're hitting them hard enough
    to kill them?"
"Just give them a good thump," said Bruce.
He snapped his elbow out of the
five gallon bucket to avoid a fin pricker.
And he showed me how to fillet
a bluegill. I started cutting carefully
and thought about the bluegill feeding frenzy
not two hours ago. Near dark, they'd bite
at anything. We lost track of just how many.
There was a heron dipping its bill and blackbirds
lining the high tension wires across the highway
drainage ponds, and greenhouses. I snagged one
by the white of its eye. So I learned
how to fillet a bluegill.
Not much meat when you finish,
but they looked good swimming around in the big
milky pot of chowder, corn and onions floating by.
I sat there at the table drinking a Pabst,
and some of the fish heads on the newspapers jawed at me,
lined up as they were, gills down,
mouth up, talking to the ceiling's bare bulb.
"What's he saying, Bruce?"
Bruce lit up a smoke.
"He's saying, 'Stop hitting me with the spoon.'"

Broken Wire

Harley worked the Winchester's lever
loading four cartridges into his rifle's magazine.
He sideswiped the table, washing gravy down
the side of the boat and sending
our six glasses of water rolling
back and forth to find a level again.

Still chewing Molly's dinner in the yard
we found secure positions near the house,
against chalked siding, our feet
sinking deep in the thickness of the weedy bank,
to watch Harley, his linen napkin tucked in
at his buckle, head directly to the paddock,
steady the gun against a tulip tree and level
the barrel at the horse's head
for what seemed a moment that never happened
when we finally righted ourselves, square again, on the legs
of Molly's caned dining room chairs.

We had to think that a man sometimes,
who bred and slaughtered cattle and hogs,
would hold a tree like the torso of a woman,
vomit down its bare trunk
worn barkless from the rubbing necks
of hard-bought breeding stock.

You have to think that a man sometimes
would not consider the weight of a dead animal
and level a rifle at the head
of his best saddle-bred stallion
dragging its own gored loop of entrails,
instead of at the bloody horn
of the bull.

By the Yew and Sweetgum

Gram forgot where Great Uncle Tom was buried,
but my mother could always remember.
He was out there by himself
away from the family
the way he would have wanted it.
A pink granite stone, mildewed,
covered with lichens in tall clumps of day lillies,
alone between two families,
an odd plot at a good price.
Monsignor O'Brien's oils stayed in the Gladstone bag
while, swearing, Tom coughed his last
through a swallow of whiskey.
His cancerous neck weeping
and bloated from holding the fiddle through
so many jigs and reels,
he was down for good.
They rolled up the carpets when Tom came after dinner
and stacked the furniture in the hall while he tweaked his
        tuning pegs.
From house to house he carried the ways
between threshing and winter,
the ways that died, settled deep
in the ticking and feathers.
"Oh, I'd forgotten all about her," says Gram
looking at the marker of a schoolmate.
With a worn cornbroom holding her up she follows
my mother, stalking the ground with a flat of impatiens
and bucket of water hauled from home.
I remember where he is,
where his ashes are washed into unconsecrated ground,
across the gravel by the yew and sweetgum.

Trout

I had to explain to her that she was as beautiful
as a trout. Not a bluegill but a trout
with brown spots finely dusted over her arms
and back. I had to explain to her that a trout was the best of fish.
Not the fish caught green over the side of a bridge
with its gasping gills, wide underslung mouth, and stomach
spewing out worm muck.
I swam with her, and I said she looked like a trout
drawn long and sleek out of a cold gravel stream. Too fine-lined
to be cut open, her own stomach, back, arms, thighs
tightly packed. Her long hair, neck, and chest
leaving the water with white skin showing off her spots
small and otherwise unseen
like on the belly of a trout,
brown against the underside of the fish, jerking
against the green grass of the bank.

Dahlias

Dahlias, we planted dahlias, digging a trench around the house.
Summers, my mother planted giant dahlias. The tubers were a gift
overflowing the brown paper bag onto the ground
under the apple trees. The blossoms were pink
and white, growing almost five inches
in diameter, and I wanted to climb
into the center and go to sleep in the curve of
one petal growing from the yellow star center.
I asked my mother to plant a blue dahlia
like the dahlia in the Raymond Chandler movie. She said
there was no such thing.
The dahlias bloomed. The fall bloomed with dahlias
along the cracked foundation.
The next year we had so many dahlias my father and I
planted them in a row
as long as the sweetcorn in the garden. And the dahlias
still came multiplying better than potatoes. If only dahlias
could be eaten. We stacked crates, winters,
in my aunt's cellar clear to the ceiling in two rows
never letting them freeze in the ground.
William Bendix went insane in Chandler's movie watching
a woman pull petals from a blue dahlia. His steel-plated skull
throbbed at the sight of the falling dahlia
petals on the glass counter reflecting the rising
dahlia petals. My aunt hated them in her cellar
adding more dirt and dahlia rot to her dirt floor.
The year my father died, we let the tubers freeze in the ground.
Leftover sprouts dried to knotted wood, or
softened, hanging through the bottom slats
of the crates. My mother would not spade a hole
or break dahlia clumps sprouted that spring. She wouldn't
stake a dahlia stalk too overgrown to stand on its own
in sandy ground that spring without my father,
a spring without dahlias.

Photo by Brad Paupore

David Marlatt lives on the farm near Richland, Michigan where he was born and raised. As well as being a writer, he is a musician who plays bass sackbut, trombone and fiddle.

Jack Driscoll is the author of a book of stories, *Wanting Only to be Heard* (The University of Massachusetts Press, 1992), and three collections of poetry, the most recent of which is entitled *Building the Cold from Memory*.